RANDOM THOUGHTS AND QUOTES OF A MIDDLE-AGED WOMAN

Brenda McCarty

PAGE PUBLISHING
Conneaut Lake, PA

First originally published by Page Publishing 2024

ISBN 979-8-89157-871-5 (pbk)
ISBN 979-8-89157-872-2 (digital)

Printed in the United States of America

Altered Path

Sometimes our lives are filled with so many obstacles that you have to literally sit down and take a breath to absorb everything coming at you. Your mind is burdened with things—what-ifs, "why didn't I," or "I should have." We all dream of a perfect life, without ups and downs. But we need bumps in the road to make us temporarily stop and observe our life and see how blessed we really are.

Approval Not Needed

Some people spend their whole life obsessing over the approval from other people. Not knowing the only approval you need is God's. Follow his commandments.

Buried Problems

Some people like to bury their head in the sand when problems arise instead of facing them head-on, not knowing that the longer they exist, the more problems you have.

Changed Emotions

In the course of a day, you run into so many people that affect you mentally, spiritually, and sometimes physically. The key to dealing with them is to let God and let go.

Cherished Memories

We should cherish those moments in our life that seem unimportant because one day they will bring you comfort and joy. We need to take time and value those moments now because one day, they will just become a faint memory.

Unsettled Souls

With the rise of gun violence, mass shooting, and racism, going anywhere feels as though we are playing Russian roulette with our lives.

What can you do?

Who will do something?

What will be done?

Pray!

Dream Big

We should encourage our children to dream big and imagine and celebrate their uniqueness in a world that sometimes seems like a carbon copy. Their uniqueness enables them to visualize extraordinary things in the simplest of things.

So be an encouragement.

Dreams Come True

When we have incidents in our life that could have altered our path, God stepped in and redirected us to our chosen purpose. God put some people on this earth for a purpose. Open your eyes to the possibilities.

What's your purpose?

Explore Your Life

Familiarity breeds contentment, and contentment breeds status quo. We need to get out of our comfort zone and experience all that life has to offer. If not, life will have passed us by, and you will be left with "I should have." Try to live every day to its fullest and enjoy the simple things.

Give Me My Flowers

Try to be the flower in someone's life. A simple compliment can uplift someone's spirit and energize their soul. Just like a bouquet of flowers will put a smile on someone's face, especially if it's unexpected. So be that flower.

Good Feeling

When you do a good deed for someone, doesn't it give you a spiritual high? Try to do a good deed every day. It will energize your soul and mind.

Good Vibes

Music is food for the spirit. When listening to music, it is like taking a temporary vacation in the mind that transports you back to a place in time where you felt free and without worries. We need to hold on to those feelings when things seem overwhelming and unchanging.

Grief Stricken

People try to tell you how to grieve, but there is no time limit on grief. If it takes you weeks or years, that's your own journey. Be assured that grief does lessen with time. But you can always reflect on the good memories of your loved one. Maybe this will lessen some of the pain.

Growing Old

As you look in the mirror, you see your pronounced wrinkles and sagging skin, and for an instant, you see a glimpse of who you were—that young woman with high hopes, dreams, and ambitions. Don't dwell in the past. Be happy with the present you because we have only one life to live, and we should live it without regret.

Happy Thoughts

Have you ever listened to a song or seen a movie or just smelled a fragrance that brought you back to a moment in time where you felt free, happy, and without worries? Hold on to those feeling when you are feeling low or distressed.

Hidden Agenda

Why do we put some people on a pedestal? Is it because of their good works, good deeds, or what? Do those people you are putting up there really deserve to be there? They have faults, flaws, and sometimes hidden agendas. Be happy with yourself because you are own best cheerleader.

Human Touch

Have we lost our humanity? Why does every bad moment become a video op, like someone falling, wearing the wrong outfit, or having a meltdown in public? We don't know what they have been through or what they're going through. We should be more empathetic and show some compassion in a world where we have lost the human touch.

I'm No Angel, Lord

God intercedes for us on so many occasions that we aren't aware of, from the smallest of things to the largest of things. When we experience that inner feeling of peace, that can only be explained as God intervening for us. So allow him to take full control.

Life Changed

Tragic events and cruel words are like a permanent stain on our soul. They linger in the mind, hidden, until something triggers them to rise. We shouldn't allow those events to mold our future or prevent us from achieving our life's goal or happiness.

Life Intervened

Obstacles are sometimes God's way of telling you to slow down, stop, and just reflect.

Lift My Load

When someone whose mind has been burdened with stress and tragedy is freed of those burdens, they radiate a glow of lightness and joy that can only be explained as God interceding.

Life Needs to Change

We sometimes go through life in an almost autopilot mode, trying to maneuver though all the obstacles we are faced with until some tragic event shocks us back into reality. We then realize that we should enjoy our life to fullest and appreciate the simple things in life.

Love Allowed

People that have been through heartbreak or betrayal form a moat around their heart, not allowing anyone to break in. We need to reopen our hearts to allow love to reenter and flourish.

Love Investment

We as women spend our whole life investing love into our spouses, children, and grandchildren and forgetting about ourselves. We need to love ourselves unconditionally and without regret for doing so.

Mind Disturbed

When living with a person with a mental disorder, it's like being on a permanent roller-coaster ride of emotions. The key to dealing with this is to relish the moments when they are good and pray when they are not.

Moments in Time

We all have past mistakes, and we wish we could push the rewind button, but there's no rewind button for life. We should treat each day as a new beginning and view it as a clean slate. We have one life to live, and we need to live it to best of our ability.

Missed Opportunity

We need to avoid letting things go unsaid because in a world where things change so rapidly, our messages could have just been a missed opportunity that could have changed someone's life.

So speak your words.

My Hero

In this age where our children put celebrities, athletes, and social media influencers on a pedestal, the greatest honor you can get is for a child to call you their hero. We need to try and live up to that title because remember, they are watching.

So be a hero!

New Beginning

Each morning you rise should be like a renewal.
New thoughts.
New ideas.
New goals.
A new you.

No Mistakes

Sometimes, life is like trial and error. Those times you get right, revel in that moment, and when you don't, avoid stressing. Remember, there is always another day.

No Regrets

As we age, every wrinkle becomes pronounced, reminding you of days gone by and the things you didn't do and making you reflect on things like "what if," "why didn't I," or "I should have." Follow your path. Be happy with yourself as your road isn't closed.

No Strangers

We as adults forget about niceties like "thank you," "please," or just saying hi to stranger. But a child, with their amazement and wonder of the world, finds a friend in every stranger they see.

Open Arms

Grandchildren are food for the soul. They energize you and give your life a purpose. So we need to nurture them, encourage them, inspire them, and most of all, feed their soul and spirit with positive energy.

Open Eyes

Some people go through life with blinders on, not being emotionally touched by anything around them until one moment, something small awakens their sense of self and purpose. Open your eyes to the possibilities.

Past Mistakes

Past mistakes are like an old movie that replay in your mind over and over and sometimes keeps you from achieving happiness and peace in your life. We need to know that those mistakes don't define you as a person and that they shouldn't attach you to the past. Live your life to fullest and without worries.

Path Not Taken

When we complain about the delays in our lives from not hearing the alarm, slow traffic, or just whatever, this just maybe God's way of slowing you down from some seen or unforeseen danger.

So don't complain!

Pay It Forward

When someone pays it forward, this gives you an overwhelming sense of goodness. Just this simple gesture can change your whole day. It encourages you to spread love everywhere you go.

So pay it forward.

Pressure Applied

Anger is like a boiling pot of water that overflows when heat continues to be applied, until that pressure gets so much it explodes like a bomb. We need to not let our emotions get to that point and try to let God take full control and direct us in the right path.

Take a breath and breathe!

Repel My Emotions

We wish our life could be water resistant, where any stresses, worries, or trauma that we may be faced with repels like water and is unable to make any permanent mark on our soul or spirit.

Rest in Peace

The death of a loved one feels like a momentary suspension of time, but without an end point. We grieve for their presence, smile, and spirit, but the loss does seem to fade away with each passing day and year. We can reflect on the memories of our loved one, and maybe this will lessen some of the pain.

Spiritual Uplift

Every once in a while, you have a profound awakening when everything seems clearer, when those stresses, worries, or problems no longer seem relevant, and that moment is when God stepped in. So allow him to take full control.

Status Quo

Why do we try to compare ourselves to other people? Are we envious of their fame, fortune, and status? We need to live the life we were given because God makes no mistakes. Be patient. God will give you everything you need.

Stories to Tell

Do you ever people watch and wonder, What's their story? Are they happy, sad, or just merely existing? People have their own story to tell. They say the eyes are the windows to the soul. View them!

Sweet Memories

Childhood memories are like a welcome friend in this chaotic world. They bring back a sense of peace and calmness in a world that is in turmoil and ever changing. We need to reflect on those memories when we feel our life is in an uproar and overwhelming.

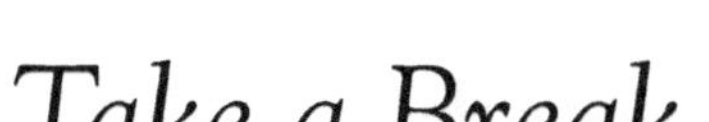

Take a Break

People have their own definition of relaxation, be it just reading a book, drinking a cup of coffee, or sitting in a quiet place, meditating. The mind is a battlefield. Each one of us needs a vacation from the mind to recharge our soul and spirit.

Rest awhile.

Troubled Mind

Stress and worry are the devil's playground. They can make your body manifest things that are not real and put your mind in overload, thinking of things that have yet to come. We don't need to be anxious about anything. Just pray about everything.

Unfinished Dreams

People always say "I meant to."
I meant to call you.
I meant to stop by to see you.
I meant to read that book.
I meant to see my relatives more often.
Don't let those "meant tos" turn into "I'm so sorry."

Unknown Path

Life is like one big mystery. You don't know from day to day what it may bring. We wait in expectations of its coming events and adjust ourselves to the reality that it brings.

Curb My Thoughts

Tragic events in our childhood sometimes follows us into adulthood like a nagging headache, sometimes impairing our ability to deal with everyday life. We shouldn't allow those events to delay our future or impair our happiness. Because everyone of us deserves to be happy.

Unseen Enemy

Depression is like an enemy you need to battle. It comes at you at your lowest point and attacks you from all sides. We need to put on the whole armor of God to reflect its draining power.

Unsettled Soul

Pent-up anger and resentment are like ticking time bombs, and you need to allow those feelings to gradually escape. If not, you will experience a massive blowout of emotions that can't be withdrawn.

Take a breath and breathe.

Unwanted Friend

Cancer is like an unwanted friend waiting around the corner to surprise you, shock you, or kill you. The key to dealing with this is to stay ready and don't let your guard down.

About the Author

Brenda McCarty is a native Texan. She is a wife, mother, and grandmother of four and a first-time author.

Her style is bohemian and nonjudgmental. Back in the day, she would consider herself a hippie and a free thinker.

Her passion nowadays is being an advocate for her grandson with special needs and enjoying retirement to the fullest.